Meet the
BUFFALO
BILLS

BY
ZACK BURGESS

NorwoodHouse Press

CHICAGO, ILLINOIS

NORWOOD HOUSE ⌂ PRESS

P.O. Box 316598 • Chicago, Illinois 60631
For more information about Norwood House Press please visit our website at
www.norwoodhousepress.com or call 866-565-2900.

Designer: Ron Jaffe
Series Editors: Mike Kennedy and Mark Stewart
Project Management: Black Book Partners, LLC.
Editorial Production: Lisa Walsh

LIBRARY OF CONGRESS CATALOGING-IN-PUBLICATION DATA
    Names: Burgess, Zack.
    Title: Meet the Buffalo Bills / by Zack Burgess.
    Description: Chicago, Illinois : Norwood House Press, [2016] | Series: Big
       picture sports | Includes bibliographical references and index. |
       Audience: Grade: K to Grade 3.
    Identifiers: LCCN 2015026323| ISBN 9781599537252 (Library Edition : alk.
       paper) | ISBN 9781603578288 (eBook)
    Subjects: LCSH: Buffalo Bills (Football team)--Miscellanea--Juvenile
       literature.
    Classification: LCC GV956.B83 B87 2016 | DDC 796.332/64074797--dc23
    LC record available at http://lccn.loc.gov/2015026323

288N—072016
Manufactured in the United States of America in North Mankato, Minnesota

CONTENTS

Words in **bold type** are defined on page 24.

The Bills leap high to celebrate a score.

4

CALL ME A BILL

The Buffalo Bills are named after Bill Cody. He was a hero of the Old West. The team and its fans have the same pioneer spirit. They love challenges. It may be getting ready for a game in the snow. Or it may be winning the championship of the National Football League (NFL).

The Bills played their first season in 1960. They were members of the **American Football League (AFL)**. After joining the NFL, the Bills played in the Super Bowl four years in a row. They have always relied on great quarterbacks, including **Jack Kemp** and Jim Kelly.

JACK KEMP
QUARTERBACK

6

Jim Kelly scans the field.

Ralph Wilson Stadium is always packed on game day.

BEST SEAT IN THE HOUSE

The Bills play in Ralph Wilson Stadium. It is named after their first owner. Bills fans come from all over New York State. Thousands also come from Canada. They meet on game day for one of America's oldest and largest tailgate parties.

SHOE BOX

The trading cards on these pages show some of the best Bills ever.

BRUCE SMITH

DEFENSIVE END · 1985-1999

Bruce had amazing speed and quickness. He had 171 **quarterback sacks** with the Bills.

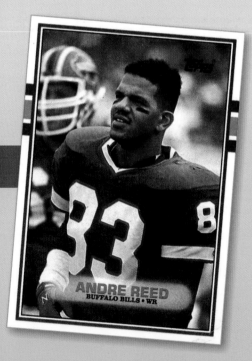

ANDRE REED

WIDE RECEIVER · 1985-1999

Andre was hard to cover, and even harder to tackle. He caught 941 passes for the Bills.

JIM KELLY

QUARTERBACK · 1986-1996

There wasn't a tougher or smarter quarterback than Jim. He led the Bills to four Super Bowls.

CORNELIUS BENNETT

LINEBACKER · 1987-1995

Cornelius was one of the team's great linebackers in the 1990s. He played in the **Pro Bowl** five times.

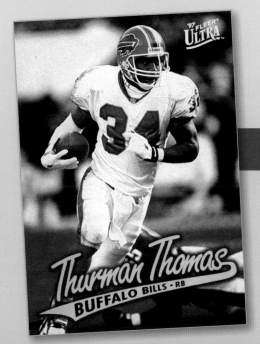

THURMAN THOMAS

RUNNING BACK · 1988-1999

Thurman was one of the most talented players in the NFL. He had a chance to score every time he touched the ball.

11

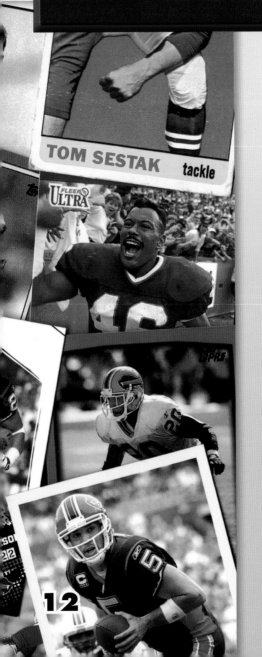

THE BIG PICTURE

TOM SESTAK   tackle

Look at the two photos on page 13. Both appear to be the same. But they are not. There are three differences. Can you spot them?

Answers on page 23.

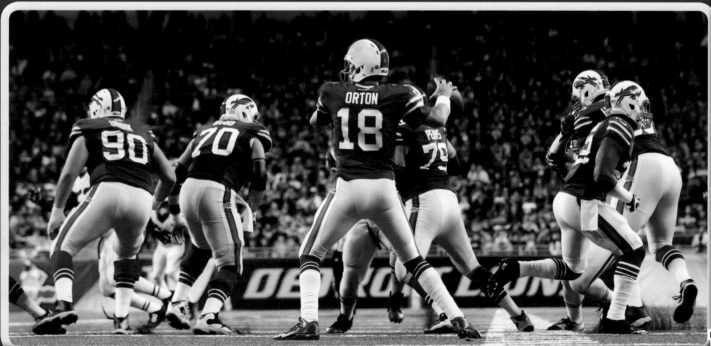

13

TRUE OR FALSE?

Mario Williams was a star defender. Two of these facts about him are **TRUE**. One is **FALSE**. Do you know which is which?

1 In 2013, Mario set a team record with 4.5 quarterback sacks in a game.

2 Mario once won a contest by eating 94 chicken wings.

3 Mario was named an **All-Pro** in 2014.

Answer on page 23.

Mario Williams sprints to break up a play.

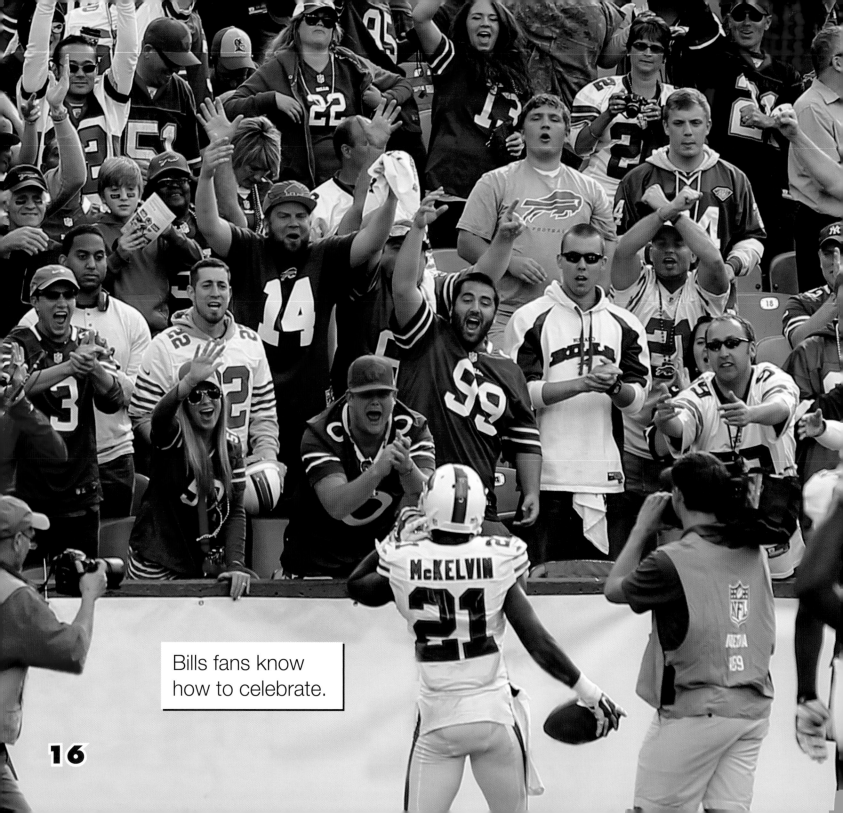

Bills fans know
how to celebrate.

GO BILLS, GO!

Bills fans are among the loudest and proudest in the NFL. After every Buffalo score, the team plays the song "Shout." The crowd always goes wild. Bills fans adored owner Ralph Wilson. When he died in 2014, they held a tailgate party at the stadium in his honor.

ON THE MAP

Here is a look at where five Bills were born, along with a fun fact about each.

1   **JACK KEMP · LOS ANGELES, CALIFORNIA**
Jack led the Bills to two AFL championships in the 1960s.

2   **STEVE TASKER · SMITH CENTER, KANSAS**
Fans loved Steve because he never gave up on a play.

3   **JOE FERGUSON · ALVIN, TEXAS**
Joe quarterbacked the Bills for 12 seasons.

4   **ELBERT DUBENION · GRIFFIN, GEORGIA**
Elbert was great at catching long passes.

5   **PETE GOGOLAK· BUDAPEST, HUNGARY**
Pete was the first of the soccer-style kickers in the 1960s.

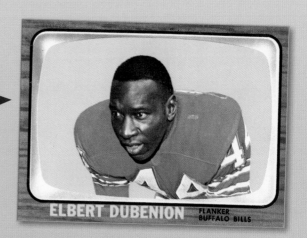

ELBERT DUBENION   FLANKER BUFFALO BILLS

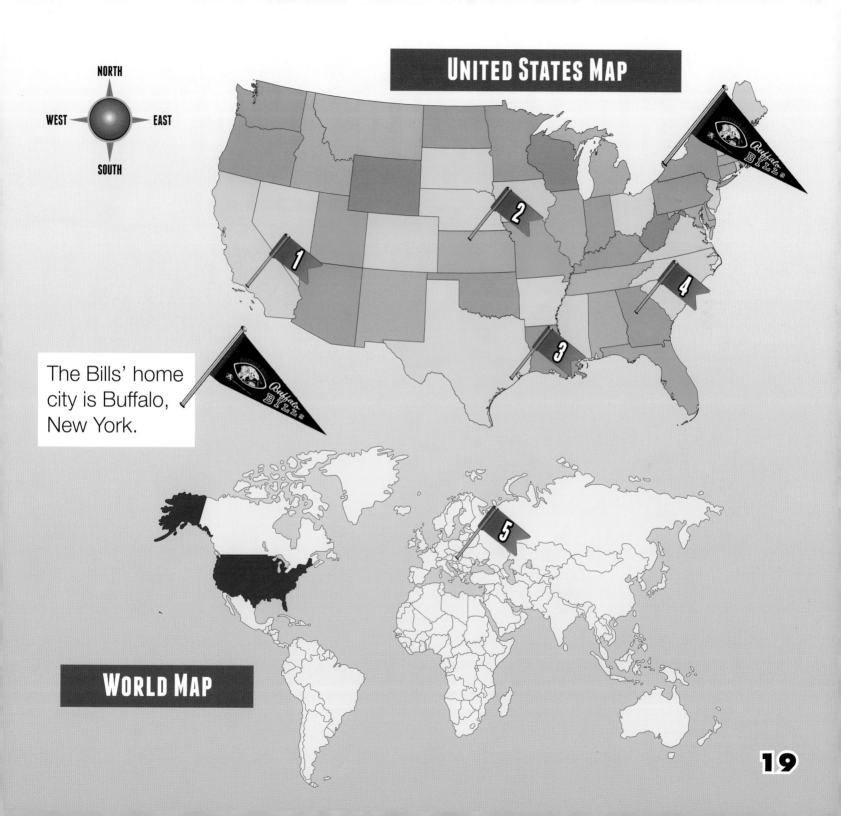

NORTH
WEST — EAST
SOUTH

UNITED STATES MAP

The Bills' home city is Buffalo, New York.

WORLD MAP

Sammy Watkins wears the Bills' home uniform.

Football teams wear different uniforms for home and away games. The main colors of the Bills are red, white, and blue. They have been the same since the team's first season.

LeSean McCoy wears the Bills' away uniform.

The Bills' helmet has a charging buffalo on each side. It is actually a picture of a bison. These animals were mistakenly identified by early settlers. The name stuck!

21

WE WON!

The Bills won two AFL titles, in 1964 and 1965. Lou Saban coached both champions. In the 1990s, the Bills made it to the Super Bowl four years in a row. No team had ever done this. Their coach was **Marv Levy**. His fast-paced offense was almost impossible to stop.

Record Book

These Bills set team records.

PASSING YARDS	RECORD
Season: Drew Bledsoe (2002)	4,359
Career: Jim Kelly	35,467

RUSHING YARDS	RECORD
Season: O.J. Simpson (1973)	2,003
Career: **Thurman Thomas**	11,938

FIELD GOALS	RECORD
Season: Dan Carpenter (2014)	34
Career: Steve Christie	234

ANSWERS FOR THE BIG PICTURE
#60 changed to #90, the logo on #18's helmet disappeared, and the goal posts disappeared.

ANSWER FOR TRUE AND FALSE
#2 is false. Mario never won a chicken wing eating contest.

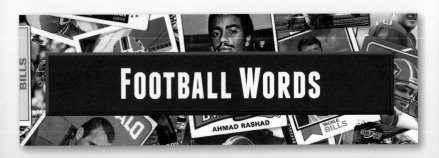

FOOTBALL WORDS

All-Pro
An honor given to the best NFL player at each position.

American Football League (AFL)
A rival league of the NFL that played from 1960 to 1969.

Pro Bowl
The NFL's annual all-star game.

Quarterback Sacks
Tackles of the quarterback that lose yardage.

INDEX

Photos are on **BOLD** numbered pages.

ABOUT THE AUTHOR

Zack Burgess has been writing about sports for more than 20 years. He has lived all over the country and interviewed lots of All-Pro football players, including Brett Favre, Eddie George, Jerome Bettis, Shannon Sharpe, and Rich Gannon. Zack was the first African American beat writer to cover Major League Baseball when he worked for the *Kansas City Star*.

ABOUT THE BILLS

Learn more at these websites:

www.buffalobills.com • www.profootballhof.com
www.teamspiritextras.com/Overtime/html/bills.html

24